SCIENCE

THE SCIENCE OF
GYMNASTICS

KATIE KAWA

PowerKiDS
press.

New York

Published in 2016 by The Rosen Publishing Group, Inc.
29 East 21st Street, New York, NY 10010

First Edition

Editor: Katie Kawa
Book Design: Katelyn Heinle

Library of Congress Cataloging-in-Publication Data

Kawa, Katie, author.
 The science of gymnastics / Katie Kawa.
     pages cm. — (Sports science)
 Includes bibliographical references and index.
 ISBN 978-1-4994-1068-6 (pbk.)
 ISBN 978-1-4994-1105-8 (6 pack)
 ISBN 978-1-4994-1137-9 (library binding)
 1. Gymnastics—Juvenile literature. 2. Sports sciences—Juvenile literature. I. Title.
 GV461.3.K39 2016
 796.44—dc23
                        2015009363

Manufactured in the United States of America

CPSIA Compliance Information: Batch #WS15PK: For Further Information contact Rosen Publishing, New York, New York at 1-800-237-9932

CONTENTS

Gymnastics is one of the most popular sports in the Summer Olympics. Every four years, people watch the best gymnasts in the world jump, flip, and take part in special exercises to win a gold medal. Young gymnasts work hard in gyms all over the world to be good enough to make their country's Olympic team.

Gymnastics is a sport that involves strength, skill, and science. Gymnasts and coaches need to understand the science behind the sport in order to be their best. Every gymnastics exercise is an example of physics at work. Physics is a branch of science that deals with the interaction between energy and matter. Gymnasts use a lot of energy when they train and compete, and physics explains how they use it.

Gymnasts take part in a series of events in every competition, and each event is an example of science in action.

GYMNASTS, LIKE ALL ATHLETES, NEED TO TAKE GOOD CARE OF THEIR BODY IN ORDER TO BE THEIR BEST. BIOLOGY IS THE BRANCH OF SCIENCE THAT DEALS WITH THE STUDY OF LIVING THINGS, INCLUDING THE HUMAN BODY. GYMNASTS NEED TO KNOW BASIC BIOLOGY IN ORDER TO AVOID **INJURIES**, BUILD STRENGTH, AND EAT THE RIGHT FOODS TO KEEP THEIR BODY IN GOOD SHAPE.

POMMEL HORSE

women's gymnastics events	men's gymnastics events
balance beam	floor exercise
floor exercise	horizontal, or high, bar
uneven bars	parallel bars
vault	pommel horse
	still rings
	vault

One of the most popular events in gymnastics is the floor exercise. During this event, gymnasts perform a **routine** consisting of flips and other tricks set to music. Tumbling passes, which are flips done in a series, make up an important part of the floor exercise. Tumbling passes begin with a gymnast running across the floor, starting from one of its corners.

When gymnasts run, they quickly change their position on the floor. The rate at which an object's position changes is known as its velocity. A gymnast's velocity increases as they run across the floor. This change in velocity is known as acceleration. Gymnasts start their tumbling passes at one corner of the floor so they have as much room as possible to accelerate.

This gymnast is increasing her velocity, or accelerating, as she runs across the floor. She needs this acceleration to help her **execute** her tumbling pass!

DIRECTION MATTERS!

VELOCITY AND SPEED MAY SEEM LIKE
THE SAME THING, BUT THERE'S AN
IMPORTANT DIFFERENCE BETWEEN
THEM. DIRECTION DOESN'T MATTER
WHEN MEASURING SPEED. HOWEVER,
IT MATTERS WHEN MEASURING
VELOCITY. THIS IS BECAUSE VELOCITY
IS DETERMINED IN PART BY HOW FAR AN
OBJECT IS FROM ITS ORIGINAL POSITION.

EXTRA POINT

Gymnasts have to stay within a set square area for the floor exercise.
This square is always 39.37 feet (12 m) long and 39.37 feet (12 m) wide.

The floor exercise is also one of the easiest places to see forces at work in gymnastics. A force is a push or pull on an object, and forces are what help gymnasts get the power they need to execute their flips. This kind of force is called applied force. An applied force is a force applied to an object, such as a gymnast's hands pushing off the floor before a flip.

While applied force helps gymnasts push themselves into the air, gravity pulls them back down. Gravity is a force that pulls objects toward the center of Earth. Gymnasts are often said to be working against gravity because they try to stay in the air as long as possible.

Gymnasts use applied force every time they push off the floor with their hands or feet in order to jump or flip.

IS IT NORMAL?

NORMAL FORCE IS ANOTHER KIND OF FORCE SEEN IN EVERY GYMNASTICS EVENT. THIS IS A FORCE ONE OBJECT **EXERTS** ON ANOTHER STABLE OBJECT IN ORDER TO SUPPORT IT. FOR EXAMPLE, THE MAT USED FOR THE FLOOR EXERCISE RESTS ON TOP OF THE FLOOR OF THE COMPETITION SITE. THE FLOOR EXERTS AN UPWARD FORCE, KNOWN AS NORMAL FORCE, ON THE MAT IN ORDER TO SUPPORT IT.

The floor used in the floor exercise isn't the same as the floors we walk on every day. It actually helps gymnasts jump higher and helps prevent injuries to their legs and feet. This is because engineers that **design** floors for the floor exercise put springs underneath the top layers of the floor.

Spring floors, such as the ones used in gymnastics, exert a kind of force called spring force on a gymnast's body. Spring force is exerted by a spring as it goes back to its original shape after being pulled or pushed down. When a gymnast jumps on a spring floor, they push springs down. The springs then push back on their feet with an upward force. This extra push helps gymnasts go higher than they could on a normal floor.

Spring floors were an important advancement in gymnastics technology. Since they were introduced, gymnasts have been able to jump higher than ever before because of spring force.

SPRING FLOORS ALSO KEEP GYMNASTS FROM GETTING INJURED, OR HURT. A SPRING FLOOR CAN **ABSORB** A GREATER IMPACT THAN A NORMAL FLOOR. IF A GYMNAST LANDED ON A NORMAL FLOOR AFTER A TUMBLING PASS, THEY COULD HURT THEIR LEGS OR FEET BECAUSE THE FLOOR WOULDN'T ABSORB THE FORCE OF THE LANDING. A SPRING FLOOR, HOWEVER, HAS SPRINGS AND LAYERS OF **MATERIAL** TO ABSORB MORE OF THE FORCE.

EXTRA POINT

Engineers are people who use math and science to make new products. Engineers are always working to make products safer for athletes, including gymnasts.

Gymnastics is a great sport to study if you're interested in kinesiology. This branch of science deals with the mechanics of body movements. One important area of kinesiology involves the way a person's body rotates, or spins, around an axis.

An axis is an imaginary line through the middle of an object. One of the axes in the human body is the transverse axis. This axis is an imaginary line running horizontally, or from side to side, through the body. A gymnast rotates around this axis when they do a somersault, or forward roll.

The longitudinal, or vertical, axis runs from the top of the body to the bottom. A gymnast rotates around this axis when they do a spin.

MULTIPLE ROTATIONS

GYMNASTS ARE KNOWN FOR EXECUTING MULTIPLE ROTATIONS AROUND ONE OF THEIR BODY'S AXES IN THE AIR BEFORE LANDING. THESE ROTATIONS ARE MEASURED IN DEGREES. ONE FULL ROTATION IS 360 DEGREES. GYMNASTS HAVE TO ROTATE THEIR BODY WITH ENOUGH SPEED TO EXECUTE MULTIPLE ROTATIONS IN THE AIR BEFORE LANDING. THEY DO THIS BY BRINGING ALL THEIR BODY PARTS AS CLOSE TO THE AXIS OF ROTATION AS POSSIBLE.

TRANSVERSE
AXIS

EXTRA POINT

Muscles are the body parts that produce motion. Gymnasts have to work hard to build strong muscles because their sport requires so many different kinds of motion.

LONGITUDINAL
AXIS

Gymnasts rotate around their transverse and longitudinal axes during most of their events, including the uneven bars, shown here.

A SIXTH SENSE

As gymnasts are tumbling across the floor or executing a flip on a narrow balance beam, they need to be aware of their body's movements and position in space. This awareness is known as kinesthetic awareness or proprioception, and it's a kind of sixth sense everyone has in their body!

Gymnasts need to always know their body's position and motion. This awareness keeps them from falling off the balance beam or hurting themselves by moving a body part incorrectly during a flip.

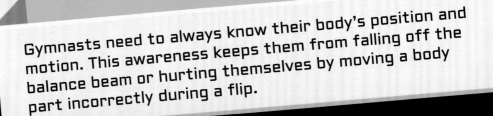

Special sensors in muscles, joints, and tendons send messages to the brain about the position and movement of these body parts. For example, these sensors send messages to the brain about the angle of the body's limbs, so the brain is aware of the body's motion. When a gymnast is in the middle of a flip, these sensors allow their brain to know the position of body parts, even when the gymnast can't see the exact position of their limbs.

MOVING TOGETHER

TENDONS AND JOINTS WORK WITH MUSCLES TO HELP ALL PEOPLE, INCLUDING GYMNASTS, MOVE. A TENDON IS A CORD THAT CONNECTS MUSCLE AND BONE IN THE BODY. A JOINT IS A PLACE IN THE BODY WHERE TWO BONES COME TOGETHER. JOINTS ALLOW BONES TO MOVE. THESE BODY PARTS WORK TOGETHER TO PRODUCE MOTION, WHICH IS WHY THEY'RE THE BODY PARTS WHERE PROPRIOCEPTORS ARE FOUND.

EXTRA POINT

The sensors that send messages to the brain about body position and movement are called proprioceptors. "Proprioception" means "sense of self."

15

Gymnasts are some of the smallest athletes in the Olympics. While many athletes are known for being tall, it actually helps gymnasts to be short. Shorter gymnasts have a lower center of gravity. A person's center of gravity is the point of their body where all their weight is **concentrated**.

A person's ability to balance is dependent on their center of gravity. This point is where the body is most evenly balanced. The lower a person's center of gravity is to the ground or to an object supporting them, the more easily they can keep their balance. This is why gymnasts bend their knees on the balance beam when they feel unsteady. That motion brings their center of gravity closer to the beam, making them more stable.

MORE MASS, MORE FORCE

GYMNASTS ARE SOME OF THE SHORTEST OLYMPIC ATHLETES, AND THEY'RE ALSO SOME OF THE LIGHTEST. THEY HAVE LESS BODY MASS THAN MOST OTHER ATHLETES. THIS IS BECAUSE OBJECTS WITH MORE MASS HAVE MORE INERTIA, WHICH IS THE RESISTANCE AN OBJECT HAS TO A CHANGE IN MOTION. THE MORE MASS A GYMNAST'S BODY HAS, THE MORE FORCE IS NEEDED TO EXECUTE THEIR FLIPS AND OTHER ROUTINE ELEMENTS.

A gymnast is able to balance more easily when their center of gravity is closer to the balance beam.

EXTRA POINT

A female gymnast's center of gravity is generally lower than that of a male because women generally carry more weight in the lower half of their body.

Gymnasts move across many different surfaces as they go through each event. A kind of force called friction exists when an object moves across a surface. Friction generally works to slow down the object's motion.

Creating friction is an important part of gymnastics. Gymnasts don't want their hands to slip off the bars, so they use sticky **substances** to create more friction between their hands and the surface of the bars. Some gymnasts use a mixture of chalk and water. Other gymnasts use honey mixed with chalk to create friction. Soda, pancake syrup, and melted gummy bears are just some of the other sticky substances gymnasts have used over the years to help them get a better grip!

BALANCE BEAM

Friction is one of the most important forces in gymnastics. It's what works to keep gymnasts from slipping off the **equipment** used for each event, which could cause injuries.

BUILDING A BETTER BEAM

THE BALANCE BEAM WAS ONCE JUST A 3.9-INCH (10 CM) PIECE OF WOOD RAISED ABOVE THE GROUND. HOWEVER, WOOD IS A SLIPPERY SURFACE, SO CHANGES WERE MADE TO THE BEAM TO CREATE MORE FRICTION BETWEEN IT AND A GYMNAST'S HANDS AND FEET. NOW, IT'S COVERED WITH LEATHER, WHICH HELPS GYMNASTS SHOW THEIR SKILLS ON THE BEAM WITHOUT SLIPPING.

EXTRA POINT

Gymnasts' hands often get sweaty as they go through each event. Sweat acts as a lubricant, which is a substance that reduces friction and makes things slippery.

CHALK

When a gymnast flips off the bars, vault, or beam, it's important for them to stick their landing. This means landing on the ground without moving. Sticking a landing isn't easy, and physics helps explain why gymnasts often keep moving after they land.

Isaac Newton, a scientist who lived from 1643 to 1727, came up with three laws of motion we still use today. Newton's first law of motion states that objects like to keep doing what they're doing. An object at rest stays at rest or an object in motion stays in motion unless acted on by an outside force.

When a gymnast's body is in motion, it wants to stay in motion. This is why stopping quickly to stick a landing takes a lot force and is not done easily.

Judges can deduct, or take away, points for not sticking a landing, but physics helps us understand why it's so hard to land without any extra motion.

EXTRA POINT

Newton's first law also states that an object in motion will want to continue with the same velocity, which is why gymnasts trying to stick their landing sometimes step in the direction they were moving before they landed.

SIZE, STRENGTH, AND MOTION

NEWTON'S SECOND LAW OF MOTION STATES THAT IF AN OBJECT IS ACCELERATING, THE ACCELERATION INCREASES WHEN THE FORCE APPLIED TO THE OBJECT INCREASES IT ALSO STATES THAT THE ACCELERATION DECREASES WHEN THE OBJECT'S MASS INCREASES. GYMNASTS COMMONLY WANT TO ACCELERATE QUICKLY, SO THEY WANT TO BE AS LIGHT AND FORCEFUL AS POSSIBLE. THIS IS WHY THEY BUILD MUSCLES WITH MAXIMUM STRENGTH AND MINIMUM SIZE.

THE PHYSICS OF THE VAULT

The vault is an event both male and female gymnasts take part in. During this event, the gymnast runs toward a piece of equipment called a vaulting table. Then, they jump onto a springboard, which allows them to push off the table with their hands. Finally, they do a number of rotations in the air before landing.

The vault is the perfect place to see Newton's third law of motion in action. This law states that for every action, there's an equal and opposite **reaction**. For example, when the gymnast jumps down on the springboard, the springboard pushes them up toward the table with equal force. Then, when their hands push down on the table, the table pushes back on their hands with an equal, upward force.

The vault is one of the easiest events to see the impact science has on gymnastics.

FROM A HORSE TO A TABLE

IN 2001, THE SHAPE OF THE EQUIPMENT USED FOR THE VAULT WAS CHANGED FROM A NARROW CYLINDER CALLED A HORSE TO THE WIDER SHAPE WE KNOW AS THE VAULTING TABLE. THIS CHANGE IN VAULT TECHNOLOGY INCREASED THE SURFACE AREA OF THE VAULT. NOW, IT'S LESS LIKELY A GYMNAST WILL MISS THE TABLE AFTER JUMPING ONTO THE SPRINGBOARD.

EXTRA POINT

The front of the vaulting table is curved downward and covered with thick padding. This is meant to prevent broken bones if a gymnast runs into the front of the table instead of jumping over it.

Gymnasts train very hard in order to be the best in their sport. They do many exercises to increase their strength and flexibility. Flexibility is a body's ability to bend easily. Gymnasts' bodies must be very flexible. They stretch, or lengthen their muscles, in order to increase their flexibility.

Gymnasts need strong muscles in order to create force and stability with their body. In order to get stronger, they do exercises that increase their muscle mass. This is called muscular hypertrophy. Gymnasts especially want to build strong muscles in their legs and shoulders. A gymnast must be careful, however, not to increase the size of their muscles too much. That would increase their overall body mass, which would make it harder to accelerate into their flips.

EATING RIGHT

EATING THE RIGHT FOODS IS JUST AS IMPORTANT TO A GYMNAST'S BODY AS DOING THE RIGHT EXERCISES. GYMNASTS NEED TO EAT FOODS THAT GIVE THEM ENERGY, HELP THEM BUILD AND HEAL MUSCLES, AND PROTECT THEIR BONES. BECAUSE OF THIS, GRAINS, PROTEINS, AND DAIRY PRODUCTS ARE IMPORTANT FOR BOTH YOUNG AND OLDER GYMNASTS.

EXTRA POINT

Flexibility in joints is called range of motion. A gymnast must have a higher range of motion in their joints than most people to execute the elements in their routines. For example, a gymnast needs a high range of motion in their hips to kick their leg as high as possible.

food group	How does this food help a gymnast?	examples of healthy foods in this group
grains	Grains provide complex carbohydrates, or substances that give a gymnast long-lasting energy.	• whole-grain bread • oatmeal • brown rice
proteins	Protein is a substance that helps build new muscles and repair muscles that have been injured.	• chicken • fish • eggs
dairy products	Dairy products contain calcium, which is a substance that helps the body build strong bones and keep bones healthy.	• milk • yogurt • cheese

This chart shows some of the foods that are important to a gymnast's diet and explains why a gymnast needs them in order to perform their best.

TECHNOLOGY IN GYMNASTICS

Technology plays a big part in helping gymnasts train. In recent years, some gymnasts started using vibration machines to increase their flexibility and height on their jumps. This kind of machine vibrates, or moves back and forth very quickly. Some gymnasts use small vibration machines to increase their flexibility. The movement produced by the machine stretches the muscles to make gymnasts more flexible. Other gymnasts stand on larger vibration machines. Studies have shown that athletes can jump higher for a short period of time after they stand on a vibration machine.

A TRAINING TOOL

GYMNASTICS COACHES OFTEN USE VIDEO TECHNOLOGY AS A TRAINING TOOL. THEY CAN SHOW A GYMNAST A VIDEO OF THEIR OWN PERFORMANCE, ALLOWING THEM TO BREAK DOWN BOTH THEIR ERRORS AND STRENGTHS. COACHES CAN ALSO SHOW YOUNG GYMNASTS VIDEOS OF ADVANCED GYMNASTS. THESE VIDEOS HELP YOUNG GYMNASTS SEE THE PROPER WAY TO EXECUTE DIFFICULT FLIPS AND OTHER SKILLS.

Technology is also used to help gymnasts prevent injuries. Gymnasts can wear sensors on their feet to show where they apply the most force when they jump. This shows places on the feet where a gymnast applies too much pressure, which could cause injuries.

EXTRA POINT

Vibration machines must be used carefully. If the vibrations are too strong, they could hurt a gymnast's body instead of helping it.

Coaches need to have a good understanding of science and technology in order to help gymnasts perform at their best and avoid injuries.

Gymnasts are awarded points and have points deducted by a group of judges for each event. After a gymnast completes an event, they're given two sets of scores. The first score is the difficulty score. Every skill is given a point value, with 0.1 being the easiest and 0.7 being the hardest. The judges then add up the points for the gymnast's hardest skills in an event, and they also include connection points for putting hard skills together.

The second score is the execution score. Judges start at 10 and then deduct points for mistakes. The highest and lowest judges' scores are thrown out, and the average score is the gymnast's execution score.

A gymnast's total score for an event is found by adding the difficulty score and execution score together.

Math plays an important part in gymnastics. A small difference in scores can make a huge difference in determining who wins a gold medal and who doesn't win a medal at all.

USING REPLAY

IF A COACH BELIEVES THE JUDGES DIDN'T AWARD THE CORRECT AMOUNT OF DIFFICULTY POINTS TO A GYMNAST, THEY CAN FILE AN INQUIRY, WHICH IS A WAY TO FORMALLY ASK THE JUDGES TO REVIEW THE GYMNAST'S ROUTINE AGAIN. THE JUDGES CAN THEN USE VIDEO REPLAY TO DETERMINE IF THE GYMNAST'S SCORE SHOULD BE CHANGED.

EXTRA POINT

A female gymnast's difficulty score is found by adding her eight hardest skills together. A male gymnast's difficulty score is found by adding up his 10 hardest skills.

Every gymnastics event is a science lesson. The floor exercise is an example of force and acceleration. The high bar and uneven bars show why friction is important. The vault is an event where Newton's three laws of motion come together. Everywhere you look at a gymnastics competition, science is at work.

Gymnasts often show off crazy skills that seem like magic. However, every skill a gymnast performs can be explained using science. The next time you watch a gymnast flip their way to a gold medal, think about the many ways science and math played a part in their success—from training to scoring. Knowing the science behind gymnastics makes the sport even more fun to watch!

STILL RINGS

GLOSSARY

absorb: To take in or soak up.

concentrated: Gathered into one area.

design: To make a plan for how to make something.

equipment: The tools needed for a certain purpose.

execute: To carry out fully.

exert: To put forth.

injury: Harm done to a person's body.

material: Something from which something else can be made.

normal: Usual or typical.

reaction: The force that an object subjected to an outside force exerts in the opposite direction.

routine: A worked-out part of an activity.

substance: Matter of a certain kind.

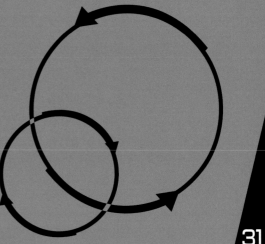

WEBSITES

Due to the changing nature of Internet links, PowerKids Press has developed an online list of websites related to the subject of this book. This site is updated regularly. Please use this link to access the list: www.powerkidslinks.com/spsci/gym